This Book Belongs to

_____

_____

Cursive Workbook for Kids

**Letter and number practice
with inspirational quotes and fun facts.**

Join Us @
www.shiviaaryandesigns.com

Cursive Letters

Trace the upper case cursive letters.

$\mathcal{A}$ $\mathcal{B}$ $\mathcal{C}$ $\mathcal{D}$

$\mathcal{E}$ $\mathcal{F}$ $\mathcal{G}$ $\mathcal{H}$

$\mathcal{I}$ $\mathcal{J}$ $\mathcal{K}$ $\mathcal{L}$

$\mathcal{M}$ $\mathcal{N}$ $\mathcal{O}$

$\mathcal{P}$ $\mathcal{Q}$ $\mathcal{R}$ $\mathcal{S}$

$\mathcal{T}$ $\mathcal{U}$ $\mathcal{V}$ $\mathcal{W}$

$\mathcal{X}$ $\mathcal{Y}$ $\mathcal{Z}$

Cursive Upper Case

Trace and write the upper case letter.

a a a a a a a a

a a a a a a a

B B B B B B B

B B B B B B B

C C C C C C C C

C C C C C C C C

Cursive Upper Case

Trace and write the upper case letter.

D D D D D D D D

E E E E E E E E

F F F F F F F F

Cursive Upper Case

Trace and write the upper case letter.

Cursive Upper Case

Trace and write the upper case letter.

J J J J J J J J

K K K K K K K K

L L L L L L L L

Cursive Upper Case

Trace and write the upper case letter.

$\mathcal{M}$ $\mathcal{M}$ $\mathcal{M}$ $\mathcal{M}$ $\mathcal{M}$ $\mathcal{M}$

$\mathcal{N}$ $\mathcal{N}$ $\mathcal{N}$ $\mathcal{N}$ $\mathcal{N}$ $\mathcal{N}$

$\mathcal{O}$ $\mathcal{O}$ $\mathcal{O}$ $\mathcal{O}$ $\mathcal{O}$ $\mathcal{O}$ $\mathcal{O}$

Cursive Upper Case

Trace and write the upper case letter.

P P P P P P P P P

P P P P P P P P

Q Q Q Q Q Q Q Q

Q Q Q Q Q Q Q

R R R R R R R R

R R R R R R R R

Cursive Upper Case

Trace and write the upper case letter.

S S S S S S S

T T T T T T T

U U U U U U U

Cursive Upper Case

Trace and write the upper case letter.

V V V V V V V V V V

W W W W W W W

X X X X X X X

Cursive Upper Case

Trace and write the upper case letter.

Cursive Letters

Trace the lower case cursive letters.

Cursive Lower Case

Trace and write the lower case letter.

a a a a a a a a

a a a a a a a a

b b b b b b b b

b b b b b b b b

c c c c c c c c

c c c c c c c c

Cursive Lower Case

Trace and write the lower case letter.

d d d d d d d d d d

d d d d d d d d d

e e e e e e e e e e

e e e e e e e e e

f f f f f f f f f f

f f f f f f f f f

Cursive Lower Case

Trace and write the lower case letter.

g g g g g g g g

h h h h h h h h

i i i i i i i i

Cursive Lower Case

Trace and write the lower case letter.

j j j j j j j j j j

j j j j j j j j j

k k k k k k k k k

k k k k k k k k

l l l l l l l l l

l l l l l l l l

Cursive Lower Case

Trace and write the lower case letter.

m m m m m m m m m

m m m m m m m

n n n n n n n n

n n n n n n n

o o o o o o o o o

o o o o o o o o o

Cursive Lower Case

Trace and write the lower case letter.

p p p p p p p p p p

p p p p p p p p p

q q q q q q q q q q

q q q q q q q q q q

n n n n n n n n n

n n n n n n n n n

Cursive Lower Case

Trace and write the lower case letter.

s s s s s s s s s

t t t t t t t t t

u u u u u u u u u

Cursive Lower Case

Trace and write the lower case letter.

Cursive Lower Case

Trace and write the lower case letter.

y　y　y　y　y　y　y

y　y　y　y　y　y　y

z　z　z　z　z　z　z

z　z　z　z　z　z　z

z　z　z　z　z　z　z

z　z　z　z　z　z　z

Cursive Letters

Trace the cursive letters.

Aa Bb Cc Dd

Ee Ff Gg Hh

Ii Jj Kk Ll

Mm Nn Oo

Pp Qq Rr Ss

Tt Uu Vv Ww

Xx Yy Zz

Connecting Letters

Trace the connecting c-o-a-d-g-q letters, then write your own.

co ca cd cg cq oc

oo ca cd cg cq oc

oa od og og ac ao

oa od og og ac ao

ad ag ag dc do da

ad ag ag dc do da

Connecting Letters

Trace the connecting n-m-v-x-y-z letters, then write your own.

nm nv nx ny nz

nm nv nx ny nz

mn mv mx my mz

mn mv mx my mz

vn vm vx vy vz

vn vm vx vy vz

Connecting Letters

Trace the connecting i-u-w-t-r-s-p letters, then write your own.

iu   iw   it   ir   is   ip

iu   iw   it   ir   is   ip

ui   uw   ut   ur   us   up

ui   uw   ut   ur   us   up

wi   wu   wt   wr   ws

wi   wu   wt   wr   ws

Connecting Letters

Trace the connecting a-e-i-o-u letters, then write your own.

ae ai ao au ea ei

ae ai ao au ea ei

eo eu ia ie io iu

eo eu ia ie io iu

oa oe oi oo ou ua

oa oe oi oo ou ua

Connecting Letters

Trace the connecting letters, then write your own.

in of to my up me

in of to my up me

as he we so be it

as he we so be it

am by or do hi ya

am by or do hi ya

Connecting Letters

Trace the connecting letters, then write your own.

ex ok yo go is as

ex ok yo go is as

oh on ma re be un

oh on ma re be un

no pa or by co he

no pa or by co he

Cursive Numbers

Trace and write your own.

1 One   1 One   1 One

2 Two   2 Two   2 Two

3 Three   3 Three   3 Three

4 Four   4 Four   4 Four

Cursive Numbers

Trace and write your own.

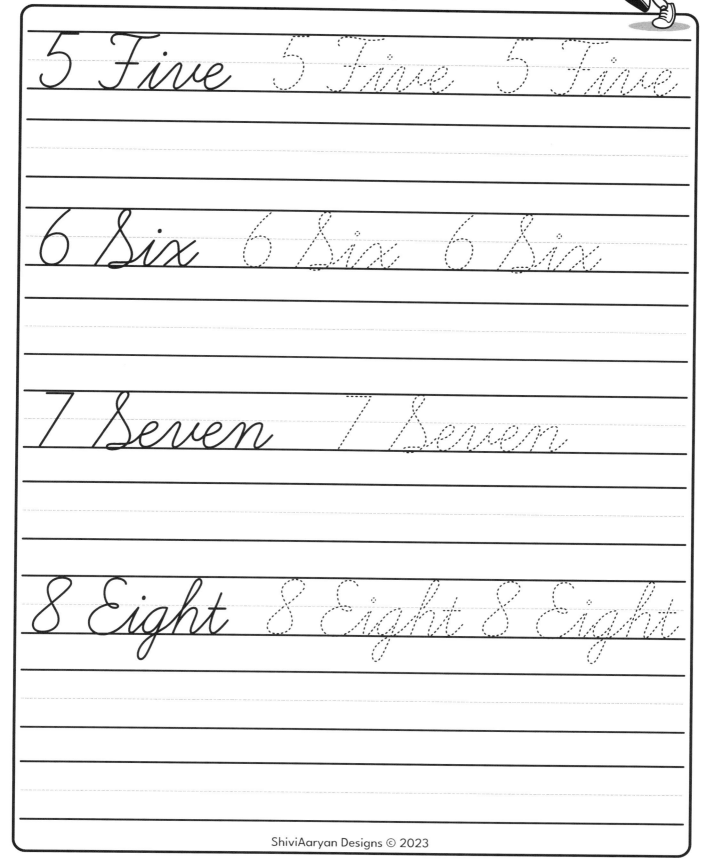

5 Five 5 Five 5 Five

6 Six 6 Six 6 Six

7 Seven 7 Seven

8 Eight 8 Eight 8 Eight

Cursive Numbers

Trace and write your own.

9 Nine 9 Nine 9 Nine

10 Ten 10 Ten 10 Ten

11 Eleven 11 Eleven

12 Twelve 12 Twelve

Weekdays

Trace and write your own.

Sunday *Sunday*

Monday *Monday*

Tuesday *Tuesday*

Wednesday *Wednesday*

Weekdays

Trace and write your own.

Thursday   Thursday

Friday   Friday

Saturday   Saturday

Sunday is a great day
doing things that make
us happy!

Months

Trace and write your own.

January *January*

February *February*

March *March*

April *April*

Months

Trace and write your own.

May *May*

June *June*

July *July*

August *August*

Months

Trace and write your own.

September September

October October

November November

December December

Colors

Trace and write your own.

Red *Red* *Red* *Red*

Green *Green* *Green*

Yellow *Yellow*

Blue *Blue* *Blue*

Colors

Trace and write your own.

Pink Pink

Brown Brown

Black Black

White White

Animals

Trace and write your own.

Dog Dog

Cat Cat

Fish Fish

Rabbit Rabbit

Animals

Trace and write your own.

Bird Bird

Mouse Mouse

Horse Horse

Cow Cow

Animals

Trace and write your own.

Pig Pig

Sheep Sheep

Lion Lion

Tiger Tiger

Animals

Trace and write your own.

Elephant Elephant

Giraffe Giraffe

Bear Bear

Monkey Monkey

Animals

Trace and write your own.

Kangaroo *Kangaroo*

Hamster *Hamster*

Turtle *Turtle*

Deer *Deer*

Magical Animals

Trace and write your own.

Unicorn *Unicorn*

Dragon *Dragon*

Phoenix *Phoenix*

Fairy *Fairy*

Magical Animals

Trace and write your own.

Mermaid Mermaid

Pegasus Pegasus

Griffin Griffin

Centaur Centaur

Magical Animals

Trace and write your own.

Basilisk Basilisk

Sphinx Sphinx

Chimera Chimera

Yeti Yeti

Magical Animals

Trace and write your own.

Minotaur *Minotaur*

Werewolf *Werewolf*

Giant *Giant*

Kraken *Kraken*

Magical Animals

Trace and write your own.

Nymph   Nymph

Satyr   Satyr

Cyclops   Cyclops

Thunderbird

Thunderbird

Dinosaurs

Trace and write your own.

Stegosaurus

Stegosaurus

Triceratops

Triceratops

Brachiosaurus

Brachiosaurus

Dinosaurs

Trace and write your own.

Velociraptor

Velociraptor

Diplodocus

Diplodocus

Ankylosaurus

Ankylosaurus

Dinosaurs

Trace and write your own.

Pterodactyl

Pterodactyl

Compsognathus

Compsognathus

Iguanodon

Iguanodon

Dinosaurs

Trace and write your own.

Deinonychus

Deinonychus

Carnotaurus

Carnotaurus

Apatosaurus

Apatosaurus

Dinosaurs

Trace and write your own.

Gallimimus

Gallimimus

Protoceratops

Protoceratops

Dilophosaurus

Dilophosaurus

Trucks

Trace and write your own.

Dump truck

Dump truck

Fire truck

Fire truck

Garbage truck

Garbage truck

Trucks

Trace and write your own.

Cement mixer truck

Cement mixer truck

Tractor trailer truck

Tractor trailer truck

Pickup truck

Pickup truck

Trucks

Trace and write your own.

Delivery truck

Delivery truck

Food truck

Food truck

Ice cream truck

Ice cream truck

Trucks

Trace and write your own.

Crane truck

Crane truck

Ambulance

Ambulance

School bus

School bus

Flowers

Trace and write your own.

Rose Rose

Lily Lily

Sunflower Sunflower

Daisy Daisy

Flowers

Trace and write your own.

Tulip Tulip

Daffodil Daffodil

Orchid Orchid

Marigold Marigold

Flowers

Trace and write your own.

Iris Iris

Carnation Carnation

Peony Peony

Geranium Geranium

Flowers

Trace and write your own.

Zinnia Zinnia

Lavender Lavender

Hibiscus Hibiscus

Poppy Poppy

Flowers

Trace and write your own.

Cosmos Cosmos

Hydrangea Hydrangea

Sweet pea Sweet pea

Chrysanthemum
Chrysanthemum

Inspirational Quotes

Trace and write your own.

"You are never too small to make a difference.

– Greta Thunberg"

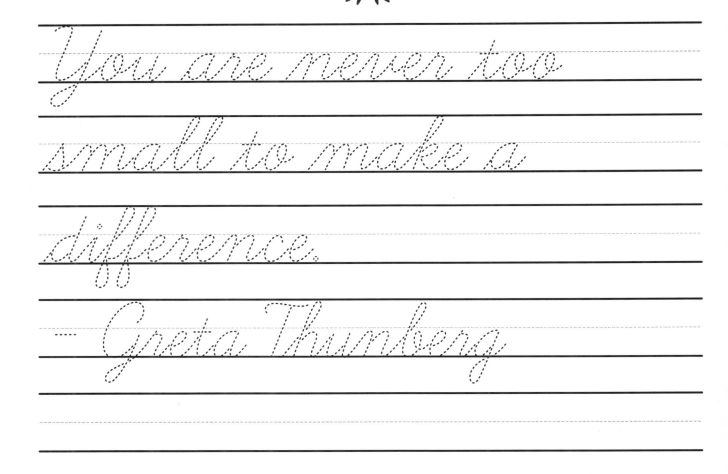

Inspirational Quotes

Trace and write your own.

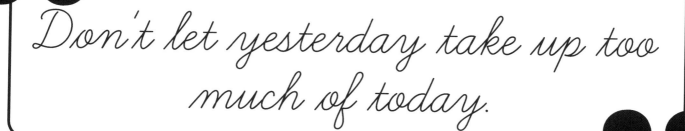

Don't let yesterday take up too much of today.

– Will Rogers

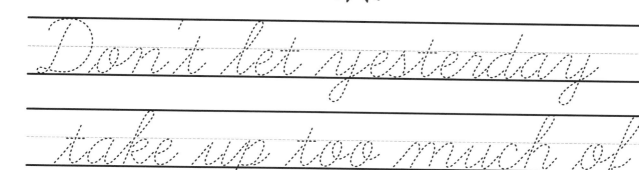

Don't let yesterday take up too much of today.

– Will Rogers

Inspirational Quotes

Trace and write your own.

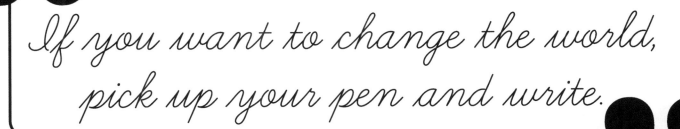

If you want to change the world, pick up your pen and write.

– Martin Luther King Jr.

If you want to change

the world, pick up

your pen and write.

– Martin Luther King Jr.

Inspirational Quotes

Trace and write your own.

> *Believe you can and you're halfway there.*
>
> — Theodore Roosevelt

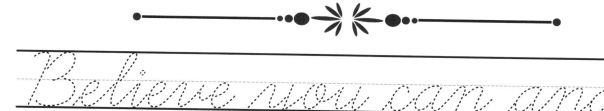

Believe you can and you're halfway there.

— Theodore Roosevelt

Inspirational Quotes

Trace and write your own.

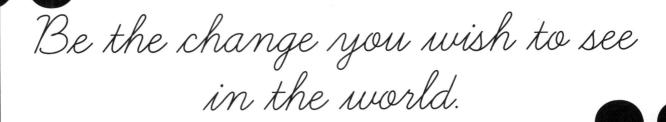

Be the change you wish to see in the world.

— Mahatma Gandhi

Inspirational Quotes

Trace and write your own.

"*It does not matter how slowly you go as long as you do not stop.*

— Confucius"

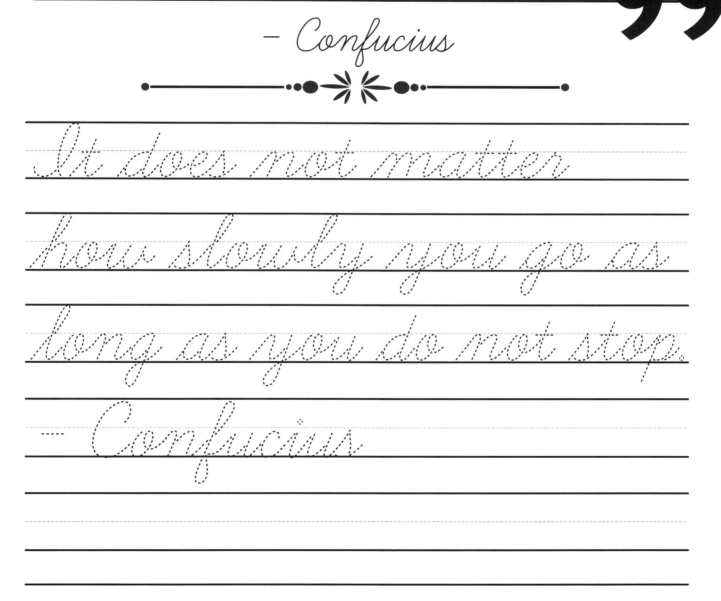

It does not matter

how slowly you go as

long as you do not stop.

— Confucius

Inspirational Quotes

Dream big, work hard, and stay focused, and you can achieve anything you want.

– Kobe Bryant

Dream big, work hard

and stay focused, and

you can achieve

anything you want.

– Kobe Bryant

Inspirational Quotes

Trace and write your own.

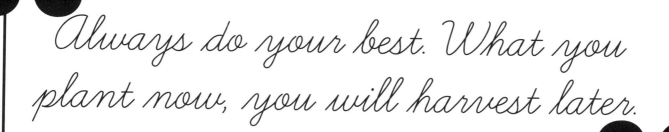

Always do your best. What you plant now, you will harvest later.

— Og Mandino

Always do your best.

What you plant now,

you will harvest later.

— Og Mandino

Inspirational Quotes

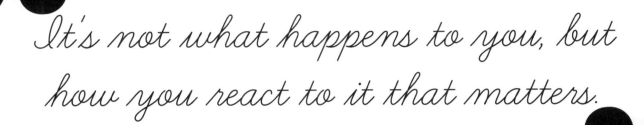

It's not what happens to you, but how you react to it that matters.

– Epictetus

It's not what happens

to you, but how you

react to it that matters.

– Epictetus

Inspirational Quotes

Trace and write your own.

> *You are braver than you believe, stronger than you seem, and smarter than you think.*
>
> *– A.A. Milne*

You are braver than

you believe, stronger

than you seem, and

smarter than you think.

– A.A. Milne

Funny Riddles

¿ Why did the tomato turn red ?

– Because it saw the salad dressing!

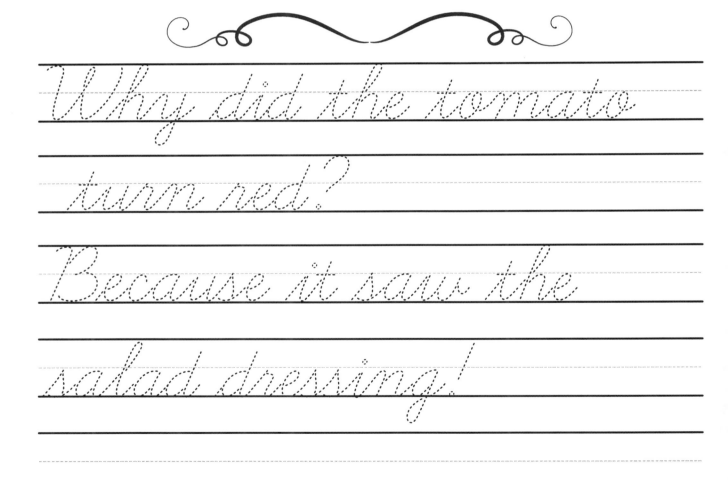

Why did the tomato

turn red?

Because it saw the

salad dressing!

Funny Riddles

Trace and write your own.

¡ What do you get when you cross a snowman and a shark ?

– Frostbite!

What do you get when
you cross a snowman
and a shark?
Frostbite!

Funny Riddles

Trace and write your own.

¿ *Why did the cookie go to the doctor* ?

– Because it was feeling crummy!

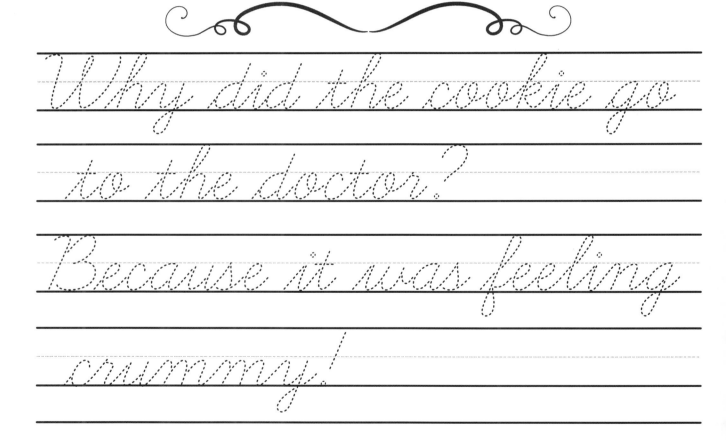

Why did the cookie go

to the doctor?

Because it was feeling

crummy!

Funny Riddles

Trace and write your own.

¿ Why did the banana go to the doctor ?

– Because it wasn't peeling well!

Why did the banana

go to the doctor?

Because it wasn't

peeling well!

Funny Riddles

Trace and write your own.

¿ Why did the chicken cross the playground ?

– To get to the other slide!

Why did the chicken

cross the playground?

To get to the other slide!

Funny Riddles

Trace and write your own.

¿ *What do you call an alligator in a vest*

— An investigator!

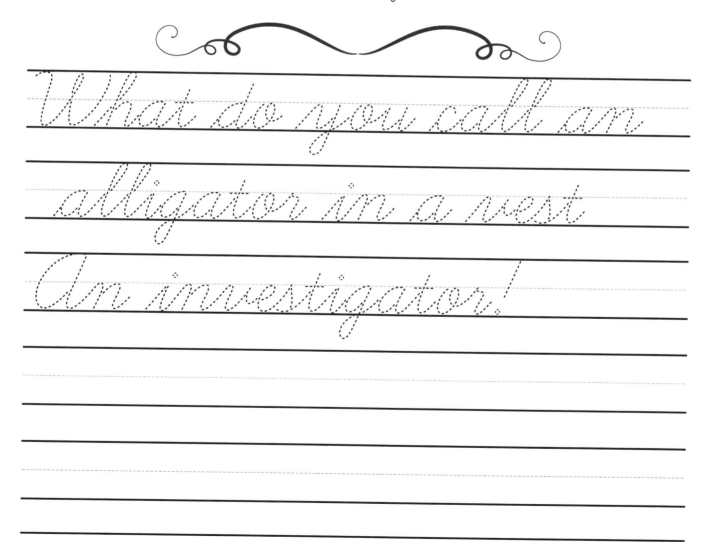

Funny Riddles

Trace and write your own.

¿ **Why did the teddy bear say no to dessert**

– *Because it was already stuffed!*

Why did the teddy

bear say no to dessert?

Because it was

already stuffed!

Funny Riddles

Trace and write your own.

¿ What do you call a fish that wears a bowtie

— Sofishticated! ?

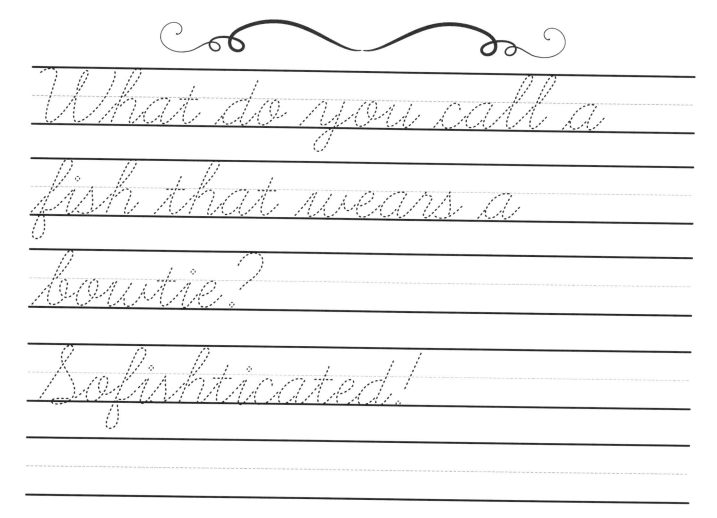

What do you call a

fish that wears a

bowtie?

Sofishticated!

Funny Riddles

Trace and write your own.

¿ Why did the banana go to school ?

– To learn how to be a-s'marter' fruit!

Why did the banana

go to school?

To learn how to be

a-s'marter' fruit!

Funny Riddles

¿ Why was the math book sad ?

– Because it had too many problems

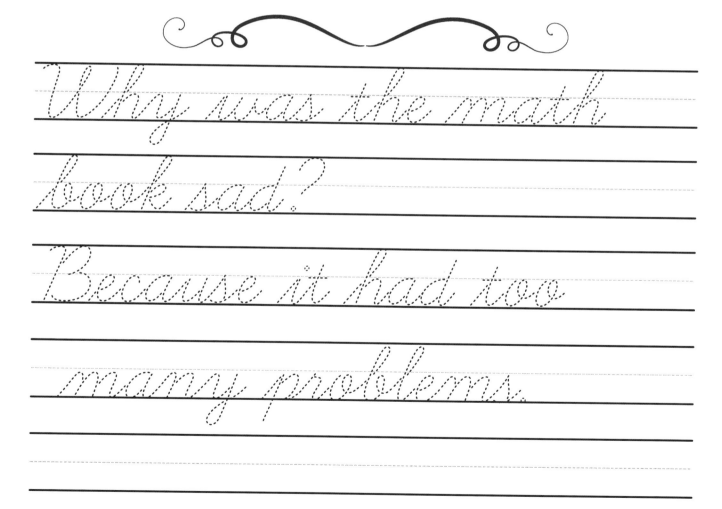

Why was the math
book sad?
Because it had too
many problems.

Fun Facts

Trace and practice writing in cursive.

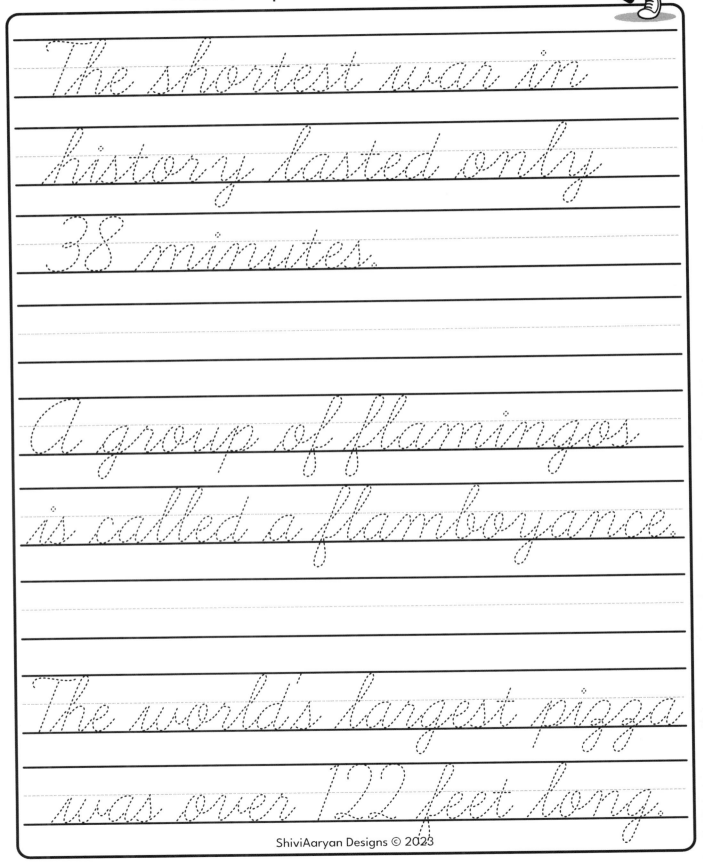

The shortest war in history lasted only 38 minutes.

A group of flamingos is called a flamboyance.

The world's largest pizza was over 122 feet long.

Fun Facts

Trace and practice writing in cursive.

Penguins can stay
underwater for up to
20 minutes.

The largest animal in
the world is the blue
whale.

Fun Facts

Trace and practice writing in cursive.

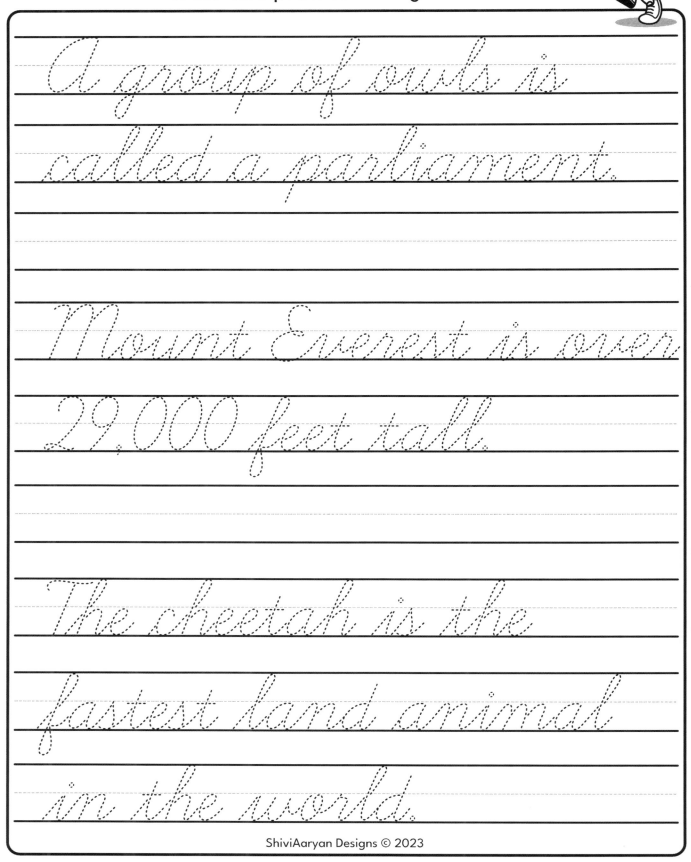

A group of owls is
called a parliament.

Mount Everest is over
29,000 feet tall.

The cheetah is the
fastest land animal
in the world.

Write Your Name

Writing about yourself in cursive

Write F&F Names

Use cursive writing to write the names of friends & family members.

School Friends

Use cursive writing to write the names of your friends at school.

Activities to do with Friends

Practice cursive writing, things that you love to do with friends.

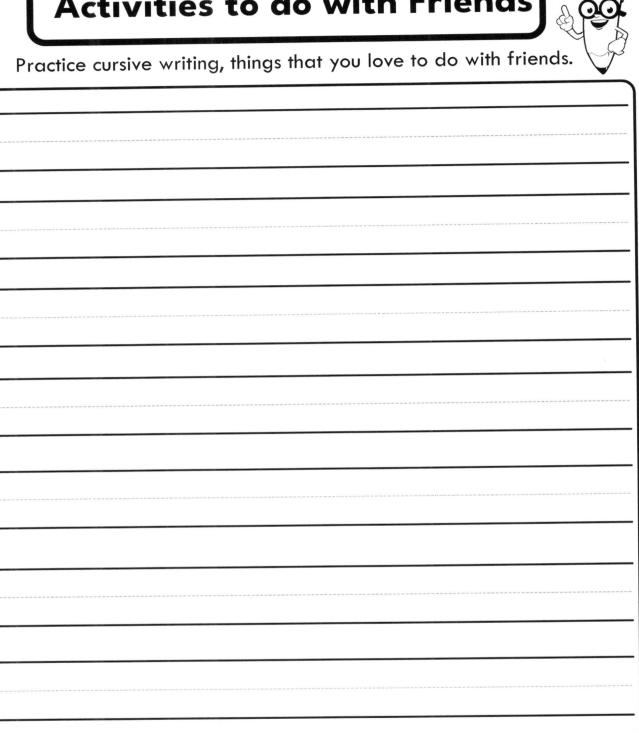

Sports like to Play

Use cursive writing, sports you like to play.

Best Teacher

Writing about your best teacher in cursive.

Practice Writing

Free cursive writing

Practice Writing

Free cursive writing

Practice Writing

Free cursive writing

Practice Writing

Free cursive writing

Practice Writing

Free cursive writing

Practice Writing

Free cursive writing

Practice Writing

Free cursive writing

Thank you for choosing this handwriting book!

We really hope you enjoyed these workbook.

Stay tuned!
We're creating new content
and other characters.

Please leave a review on the Amazon website

Thank You!

Made in the USA
Middletown, DE
01 October 2023

39899656R00057